AIDS: First Facts for Kids

Written by Linda Schwartz
Illustrated by Denise Clemmensen

The Learning Works

Cover Design by Pro-Graphics

Illustrations by Denise Clemmensen

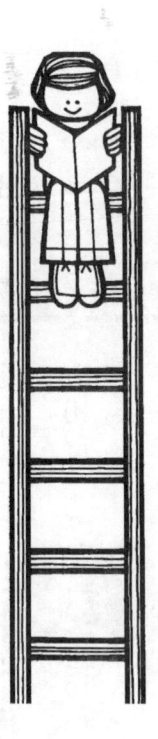

Typesetting and Editorial Production by Clark Editorial & Design

---

Acknowledgments

Special thanks to Ronald M. Ferdman, M.D., Division of Clinical Immunology and Allergy at Childrens Hospital Los Angeles and Assistant Professor of Clinical Pediatrics at the University of Southern California, and to Dr. Cary Savitch, author of *The Nutcracker is Already Dancing*, for their expertise and insightful comments on the manuscript.

The purchase of this book entitles the individual teacher to reproduce copies for use in the classroom. The reproduction of any part for an entire school or school system or for commercial use is strictly prohibited. No form of this work may be reproduced, transmitted, or recorded without written permission from the publisher. Inquiries should be addressed to the Permissions Department.

Copyright © 1997
The Learning Works, Inc.
P.O. Box 6187
Santa Barbara, California 93160

ISBN: 0-88160-249-3

Contents

A Note to Parents and Teachers 5
Introduction 6

All About HIV/AIDS
What is AIDS? 7
What causes AIDS? 8
When was HIV/AIDS first reported? 9
Who can get HIV/AIDS? 10
Did You Know? 11

How HIV is Spread
What are some wrong ideas about HIV/AIDS? 12–13
What about AIDS and sex? 14
What about AIDS and drugs? 15
What are other ways HIV is spread? 16
Is it safe to be around a classmate with HIV? 17
Can a person get HIV by kissing? 18
Can someone get HIV from playing sports? 19
Can a person get HIV from a blood transfusion? 20
Did You Know? 21

Understanding HIV/AIDS
Can people tell right away if they have been infected with HIV? 22
How do people find out if they have HIV? 23
What happens after a person becomes infected with HIV? 24
How do doctors tell if HIV has progressed to AIDS? 25
What are some of the symptoms of AIDS? 26
Do people with HIV always get AIDS? 27
Did You Know? 28

HIV/AIDS Prevention
Can HIV be prevented? 29
What does alcohol and drug use have to do with HIV? 30
What steps can you take to stay healthy? 31
How can people reduce their risk of getting AIDS? 32
What Would You Do? 33
Design a Postage Stamp 34
Topics to Debate 35
Did You Know? 36

AIDS: First Facts for Kids
© The Learning Works, Inc.

Contents

HIV/AIDS Treatments
What should people do if they test positive for HIV? 37
Is there a cure for AIDS? 38
What drugs are available to treat HIV/AIDS? 39
Did You Know? 40–41

Profiles and Feelings About HIV/AIDS
People in Profile 42
How does society treat people who have HIV/AIDS? 43
What can you do to help someone with HIV/AIDS? 44–45
How have your feelings changed? 46

Extended Activities to Learn More About HIV/AIDS
Word Search Puzzle 47
The AIDS Quilt 48
An AIDS Review 49
Research Projects 50
Creative Writing and Art Ideas 51
Role-Playing Activities 52
Cooperative Projects 53

HIV/AIDS Information Resources
Books to Read 54
Resources for More Information 55–56

AIDS: First Facts for Kids
© The Learning Works, Inc.

A Note to Parents and Teachers

No one book can be all things to all students, especially when dealing with such controversial issues as HIV, AIDS, and sexuality. The material in this book is written specifically for students in grades 4–6. Some students in these grades may be ready to handle information about HIV/AIDS in greater depth and detail. For those students, a list of resources has been provided on pages 55 and 56 which provides the names of organizations and foundations that will be glad to send free literature and information.

In addition, the books *AIDS: Answers to Questions Kids Ask* and *AIDS: What Teens Need to Know*, published by The Learning Works, are available for teenagers. These activity books address issues of interest to the more mature student and include discussions of such topics as drug abuse and sexuality.

The facts contained in this book reflect the understanding about HIV/AIDS at the time of publication. Because information about HIV/AIDS is increasing and changing rapidly as research reveals new facts, this book will be updated periodically so that the ideas presented are both current and relevant to young people.

Introduction

At this stage of your life, your days are filled with family, friends, school, sports, and many outside interests and activities. You are probably wondering, "Why should I worry about AIDS?"

You need to be concerned about AIDS because this disease almost always results in death and because you are potentially at risk for this disease. In a short time, the AIDS epidemic has become a major health crisis, and scientists expect AIDS to continue to spread. As of this writing, there is no vaccine to prevent AIDS and no medicine to cure it. It is important to remember, however, that AIDS can be prevented. Educating yourself about AIDS is the first step towards preventing this disease.

The purpose of *AIDS: First Facts for Kids* is to make you aware of the facts about AIDS, a disease caused by a virus. It is important for you to learn how this virus is spread and how to prevent its transmission. Also, in becoming better informed, you will enable yourself to make intelligent and responsible decisions regarding your personal behavior now, as a teenager, and as a young adult.

Many new terms related to AIDS are introduced in this book. You will find pronunciations and definitions of these words at the bottom of each page when the words are first introduced. Also, many pages contain extended activities that you can do if you want to learn more about AIDS.

What is AIDS?

AIDS is an acronym made up of the first letters of the words **acquired immune deficiency syndrome**. This acronym names a disease that attacks the body's immune system.

The immune system is the part of the body that protects us from getting infected with germs (like viruses or bacteria) and helps the body get rid of or cure these infections once they start. The immune system is made up of many parts, many of which are in the blood. Our blood is filled with cells. Most of these are red cells (that is why blood looks red), but some are white blood cells. White blood cells are an important part of the immune system because they produce antibodies—substances which attack and weaken or kill invading germs. Every time a germ enters the body, antibodies are produced in an effort to fight the germ. A person infected with the virus that causes AIDS will make antibodies, but unfortunately these antibodies are not strong enough to cure the infection.

When you have a cold or the flu, you are sick for awhile and may not feel well. But eventually you get better because your body's immune system fights and destroys the germs that are causing the illness. A person who has AIDS cannot fight infections well because the virus has damaged his or her immune system. A person who has AIDS will get sick again and again and will have trouble getting well.

New Words

acquired	(a-kwy-erd) adj.: gotten as a result of exposure, experience, or environment rather than heredity.
deficiency	(de-fish-en-see) n.: a shortage or lack.
immune	(i-myoon) adj.: protected; able to resist to disease.
syndrome	(sin-drome) n.: a combination of specific symptoms indicating the presence of a disease.

Q What causes AIDS?

A AIDS is caused by a virus known as **HIV**, an acronym that stands for **human immunodeficiency virus**. This virus is found mainly in blood, **semen**, and fluids in the vagina. The virus can also be found in other body fluids such as saliva, intestinal secretions, and tears, but in much smaller quantities.

A person can have HIV and not show any disease **symptoms** at all. For this reason, infected people may not be aware that they are carrying the disease and may **infect** others without knowing it.

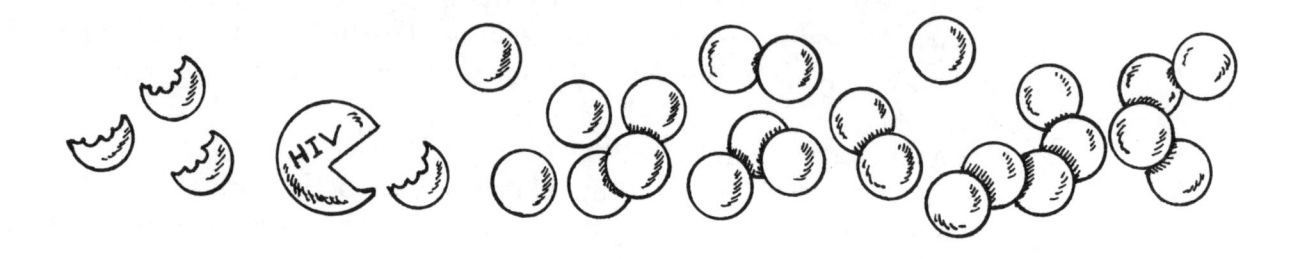

New Words

infect (in-fekt) v.: to cause someone to catch a disease.

semen (se-men) n.: the whitish fluid that is produced by males during sexual activity and contains male reproductive cells.

symptom (sim-tem) n.: something you can see or feel that indicates the presence of a disease. For example, fever, pain, and swelling are all symptoms.

virus (vi-rus) n.: a microscopic disease-producing agent that depends on other cells for its growth and reproduction. The common cold, chicken pox, flu, and polio are diseases that are caused by viruses.

AIDS: First Facts for Kids
© The Learning Works, Inc.

Q A

When was HIV/AIDS first reported?

HIV/AIDS was first reported in the United States in 1981. As of December, 1996, more than 581,429 cases of AIDS have been reported in the United States to the Centers for Disease Control in Atlanta, Georgia. The Centers for Disease Control is a government agency that is responsible for keeping track of and studying important diseases.

The World Health Organization states that as of December, 1996, more than 30 million people worldwide have been infected with HIV.

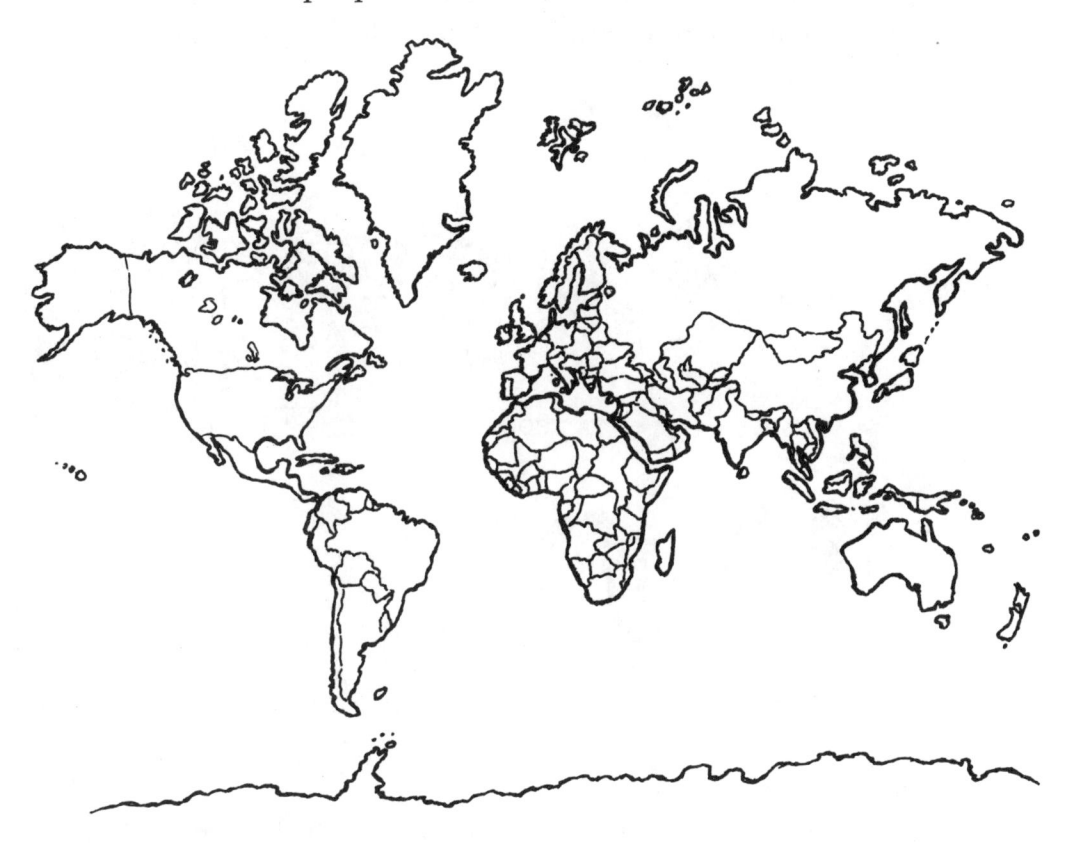

On Your Own

Working independently, researchers Dr. Luc Montagnier from France and Dr. Robert Gallo from the United States discovered the virus that causes AIDS. Today, scientists are searching for ways to prevent and cure this disease. Do some research to find out what scientists have learned recently about AIDS. For up-to-date information, look in medical journals, magazines, and newspapers. You can also check the Internet for information about HIV/AIDS at the following Web sites:

http://www.cdcnac.org
http://www.aacap.org/web/aacap/factsFam/aids.htm
http://www.ryanwhite.org/

AIDS: First Facts for Kids
© The Learning Works, Inc.

Q. Who can get HIV/AIDS?

A. Anyone...

males and females

heterosexuals and homosexuals

people of all races and religions

the rich and the poor

the very young

and the very old

However, research today shows that the presence of infection is highest among homosexuals, intravenous drug users, and people with multiple sex partners.

New Words

heterosexual   (het-er-o-sek-shoo-ul) n.: a person showing sexual preference for another person of the opposite sex.

homosexual   (ho-mo-sek-shoo-ul) n.: a person showing sexual preference for another person of the same sex.

AIDS: First Facts for Kids
© The Learning Works, Inc.

Did You Know?

- About every 10 minutes, a person in the United States becomes infected with HIV.

- No one knows for sure where the AIDS virus originally came from.

- The Centers for Disease Control and Prevention keeps track of the numbers of HIV and AIDS cases in the United States. Doctors in all states are required by law to report AIDS cases. Although many states also report HIV cases, they are not required to do so. This means that a lot of people already infected with HIV are not reported and counted by the Centers for Disease Control.

- A person infected with the AIDS virus is said to be "HIV-positive."

- Once someone is infected with HIV, he or she remains infected for life.

- About 362,000 people in the United States have died from AIDS-related diseases since the first-known cases were discovered in 1981.

- People who have AIDS do not actually die from AIDS itself but from other illnesses such as cancer, pneumonia, and other infections.

- Information gathered by the Centers for Disease Control show that HIV infection is increasing among teens.

- About one-fourth of people with AIDS are drug abusers who use hypodermic needles to inject drugs such as cocaine and heroin.

- Doctors don't know why some people with HIV develop AIDS more quickly than others.

- During the early years of infection, it is impossible to tell if a person has HIV by how he or she looks. The only way to know if someone is HIV-positive is by testing.

- The virus that causes AIDS is hard to study. It takes on many different forms, changes the way it looks and moves, and also changes the body cells it attacks.

AIDS: First Facts for Kids
© The Learning Works, Inc.

Q&A What are some wrong ideas about HIV/AIDS?

Some **wrong** ideas about HIV/AIDS are that you can catch the virus

by touching a person with HIV/AIDS

from a toilet seat

from a hug

from a drinking fountain

What are some wrong ideas about HIV/AIDS? (continued)

Some **wrong** ideas about HIV/AIDS are that you can catch the virus

by breathing the air

by eating in a restaurant

by using the telephone

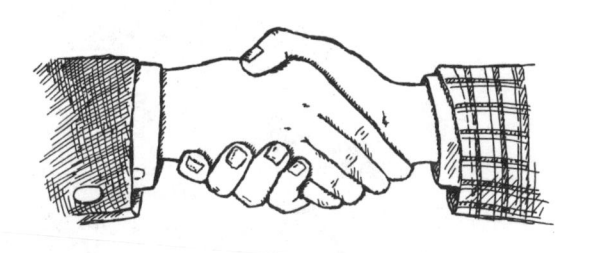

or by casual contact at home, in school, at play, or at work

Research has shown that you are **not** likely
to get the virus in any of these ways.

AIDS: First Facts for Kids
© The Learning Works, Inc.

What about AIDS and sex?

Before a virus can make you sick, it must find its way into your body. The primary way in which AIDS is acquired and **transmitted** is by intimate sexual contact. HIV, the virus that causes AIDS, is found in blood, semen, and vaginal fluids. It is also found in saliva and breast milk, but in much smaller amounts. During **sexual intercourse**, this virus may penetrate the thin skin of the vagina or penis through tiny breaks or cuts. Once the virus has entered the bloodstream, it attacks and changes disease-fighting blood cells. In this way, HIV permanently cripples the immune system and leaves the body unable to fight off the infections that eventually lead to AIDS.

AIDS cannot be cured, but it can be prevented. Because HIV is transmitted during sexual contact, the spread of the disease can be controlled by changes in personal behavior. Faced with the risk of HIV infection, many teenagers are deciding to postpone having sexual intercourse until they are emotionally ready to make a long-term commitment to one person. These commitments result in marriage and in relationships in which neither partner has sexual intercourse with anyone else. Individuals must also consistently take the precautions necessary to prevent the spread of HIV. The first step is to learn about HIV and AIDS. HIV educators at family planning centers and local health departments can provide more information about how individuals can protect themselves from HIV.

New Words

sexual intercourse (in-ter-korse) n.: physical sexual contact.

transmit (tranz-mit) v.: to send, pass, or cause to go from one person to another.

Q&A What about AIDS and drugs?

People who give themselves **intravenous** or **intramuscular** injections of drugs risk getting AIDS if they share needles. Researchers estimate that approximately 25% of all people with AIDS probably became infected through needle-sharing. When a person infected with HIV injects drugs with a needle, tiny amounts of his or her infected blood may be drawn into the needle and syringe. When another person uses the same needle, the virus may be transmitted to this second user. Because people can carry and transmit HIV without showing any symptoms, sharing needles is never safe. One use of a **contaminated** needle may be all it takes to become infected with HIV for life. A person who has sexual intercourse with someone who injects drugs can also become infected.

The needles used in clinics, hospitals, and doctors' offices are not contaminated. When you receive a shot from a doctor or nurse, the syringe has been carefully sterilized to kill any harmful germs. A disposable needle is used and then both the syringe and the needle are thrown away after the shot. But illegal drug users usually do not sterilize or discard their needles or syringes after use. Instead, they often keep and share them.

New Words

contaminated (ken-tam-uh-na-ted) adj.: made dirty or impure by the introduction of some foreign or undesirable substance.

intramuscular (in-tra-mus-cue-lar) adj.: entering the body by means of a muscle.

intravenous (in-tra-vee-nus) adj.: entering the body by means of a vein.

AIDS: First Facts for Kids
© The Learning Works, Inc.

What are other ways HIV is spread?

Besides sexual contact and sharing intravenous drug needles, there are other ways HIV can enter the body. These ways do not occur very often, but it is important to be aware of them.

- Instruments used for acupuncture, tattooing, and any kind of body piercing such as ear or nose piercing can transmit HIV if they are used on an infected person and then reused on another person. If you get your ears pierced, make sure that only new, sterilized, packaged needles are used.

- Don't share personal items such as toothbrushes, razors, tweezers, or scissors. There is a slight risk of HIV infection if blood from a person infected with HIV remains on these items after use. This is especially important if you have a cut or sore that the blood might come in contact with.

- HIV can be transmitted from a mother's bloodstream into her unborn baby's bloodstream, or from her breast milk into her newborn baby's bloodstream.

AIDS: First Facts for Kids
© The Learning Works, Inc.

Q Is it safe to be around a
A classmate with HIV?

Yes. It is safe to be around a classmate with HIV. You should not be afraid to work together on group projects, sit together at lunch, play together at recess, or be in close contact. You cannot catch HIV/AIDS the way you catch a common cold. Nor can you become infected with HIV from things you do at school each day, such as using the restroom, drinking from a water fountain, or standing close together in line. Unless you are sharing drug needles or having unprotected sex, you are not at risk for becoming infected with HIV.

A classmate with HIV is actually putting himself or herself at risk by attending school. His or her immune system has already been weakened by the virus. This leaves him or her open to any diseases, infections, or viruses that other classmates might have.

On Your Own
Put yourself in the shoes of a person your age who is infected with HIV. Think about what your life would be like at school. Do you think your classmates would support you and show compassion? Would they invite you to play in their games and work on class projects together? Write a journal entry describing your experiences at school on a typical day as a student with HIV.

AIDS: First Facts for Kids
© The Learning Works, Inc.

Q&A Can a person get HIV by kissing?

A person cannot get HIV/AIDS from a friendly kiss on the cheek. However, because small traces of the virus have been found in saliva, there is a slight risk of getting HIV/AIDS by French kissing (where one person puts his or her tongue in another person's mouth), especially if either person has open sores inside or around the mouth. Although the risk is small, there has been a documented case of HIV being spread by kissing, and there may be other cases that have not been reported.

One of the ways HIV is transmitted is by blood. The risk of HIV increases if any blood is present during kissing due to a cut or sore on the lips or mouth, or if an infected person has bleeding gums. Again, the risk is very small, but it is a still a possibility.

On Your Own — Create a thirty-second television commercial to make people more aware of AIDS and to educate them regarding the ways in which this disease is transmitted. Write a script for your commercial in which you include the words you'll say and the visual effects you will use. Memorize your script and present your commercial to your classmates. If possible, videotape your commercial.

AIDS: First Facts for Kids
© The Learning Works, Inc.

Q&A: Can someone get HIV from playing sports?

According to studies done by the Centers for Disease Control, the risk of getting HIV/AIDS as a result of a sports injury is extremely low. When you participate in sports, however, it is wise to take certain precautions. Always report injuries involving blood to a parent, a teacher, a coach, or other adult so he or she can administer the appropriate first-aid. Never touch blood that isn't your own.

On Your Own

Do research to find out basic first-aid procedures for each of the following mishaps that can occur while participating in sports activities:

- a nosebleed
- sand or dirt in your eyes
- a sprained finger
- a black eye

AIDS: First Facts for Kids
© The Learning Works, Inc.

Q / A Can a person get HIV from a blood transfusion?

A blood transfusion is a procedure in which the blood of one person is transferred to another person. This might be done, for example, when a person is in the hospital and needs to be given blood during an operation. Today, blood transfusions are safer than in the past. Before 1985, the nation's blood supply could not be screened, or tested, for HIV antibodies. During this time, some people received the virus in transfused blood.

In March of 1985, a test was developed to screen blood. Since that time, all donated blood has been carefully tested. Any blood that tests positive is discarded and is not used in the preparation of blood products or for transfusions. For these reasons, you are unlikely to get HIV/AIDS from a blood transfusion.

On Your Own

Hemophilia is a hereditary condition in which the blood fails to clot properly. *Hemophiliacs*, or persons suffering from hemophilia, bleed easily and need frequent transfusions of whole blood or blood products to help their blood clot more readily or to replace blood they have lost.

Do research to learn what other conditions and diseases are sometimes treated by means of transfusions.

AIDS: First Facts for Kids
© The Learning Works, Inc.

Did You Know?

- You cannot get HIV from animals because they cannot transmit the disease.

- You cannot get HIV from insects that suck blood, such as ticks or mosquitoes. They can draw blood out of your body but can't inject it back into another person's body.

- People who donate blood cannot get HIV because they are not coming in contact with another person's blood. Blood banks use sterilized equipment and needles that are used just one time and then thrown away.

- Unlike a cold virus, HIV is not spread through coughing or sneezing.

- Using an infected drug needle or syringe just one time can transmit HIV.

- People who have sex with many partners increase their risk of getting HIV and of spreading the virus to others.

AIDS: First Facts for Kids
© The Learning Works, Inc.

Q&A Can people tell right away if they have been infected with HIV?

No. One special characteristic of this virus is its ability to stay alive in the body for weeks, months, or even years before causing symptoms.

Sometimes, a few weeks after people have become infected with HIV, they may experience symptoms that resemble the flu. These symptoms can include fever, chills, diarrhea, swollen glands, or headaches. Other people may be infected with HIV and not show any of these symptoms.

Q A How do people find out if they have HIV?

The most common way doctors determine if people have HIV is by checking their blood for the presence of HIV antibodies.

After HIV enters the bloodstream, the body begins producing special proteins called antibodies in an effort to weaken and destroy the virus. The presence of these antibodies in a blood sample indicates that the patient has been infected with HIV. To make this determination, a blood test is given and the blood collected is examined to see if HIV antibodies are present. If they are, the test results are said to be *positive*. If no HIV antibodies are found in the blood samples, the test results are said to be *negative*. The person is considered to be free of HIV.

In some cases, the blood of a person infected with HIV will test negative even though the person has HIV. This is because his or her body has not yet started producing antibodies. Sometimes it takes two weeks to six months before the body produces antibodies. Therefore, a repeat test is required three to six months after the first test to be sure the results are correct.

AIDS: First Facts for Kids
© The Learning Works, Inc.

Q/A: What happens after a person becomes infected with HIV?

After the initial infection, a person with HIV usually has no symptoms for months or years. He or she is said to be *asymptomatic*. The person has been infected with HIV but doesn't show any symptoms of the infection. This period can last anywhere from 2 to 15 years after the initial infection. The average length of time between infection with the virus and the appearance of symptoms that can be identified is about 7 to 10 years. *The person can still pass the virus to other people even when he or she is asymptomatic.* Also, even though a person is asymptomatic, the virus is slowly attacking and weakening his or her immune system.

As the disease progresses and more damage is done to the body's immune system, other problems occur. People infected with HIV at this stage may have lung, skin, and intestinal infections that occur over and over. Sometimes they have high fevers that last for days. They may have a long-lasting white coating in their mouth or heavy sweating at night. Other symptoms of HIV infection are sores or infections that don't respond to treatment, swollen glands, and a cough that lasts for weeks. This stage is sometimes called "HIV illness."

If a person has one or more of these symptoms, it doesn't always mean he or she has been infected with HIV because other diseases cause similar symptoms. The only way for a person to know if he or she is infected is to be tested.

AIDS: First Facts for Kids
© The Learning Works, Inc.

How do doctors tell if HIV has progressed to AIDS?

One of the main ways that doctors can tell if a person with HIV has progressed to having AIDS is by testing his or her blood to count the person's CD4-cells. CD4-cells are the most important type of T-cells, called "helper" T-cells. T-cells are important because they control many other parts of the immune system. A *CD4-cell count* is a test that lets a doctor see how many helper T-cells a person has in his or her blood. This count helps doctors monitor a patient's response to treatment for HIV. It also shows the progression of HIV infection in the body.

As HIV infection increases, a person's CD4-cell count gets lower and lower because the healthy cells are being destroyed by the virus. When this happens, a person's ability to fight off infections is decreased. The immune system is suppressed or weakened. This condition is known as *immunosuppression*—a term which comes from the words *"immune"* and *"suppression."*

An adult with a healthy immune system usually will have a CD4-cell count of 600 to 1,500. As immunosuppression continues, the CD4-cell count drops. At a certain point, **opportunistic infections** develop because the immune system is too weak to fight off infections. According to the Centers for Disease Control, an adult with a CD4-cell count of less than 200 is considered to have AIDS, even if they do not yet have any symptoms.

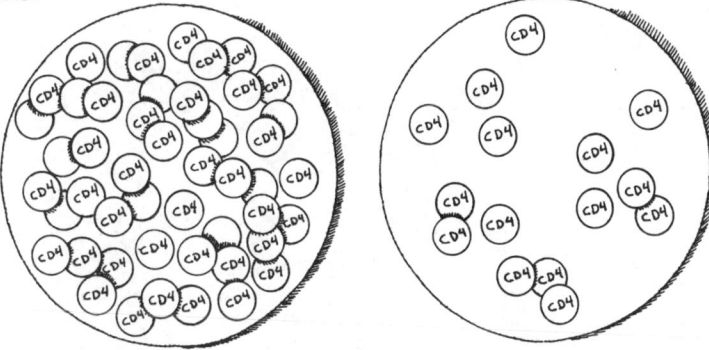

New Words

opportunistic infection (OI)	(ah-per-too-nis-tik in-fek-shun) n.: infection by one of the many germs which usually do not cause illness in a healthy person, but which can cause severe illness in a person with a weak immune system.

AIDS: First Facts for Kids
© The Learning Works, Inc.

Q What are some of the symptoms of AIDS?
A

In addition to a CD4-cell count of less than 200, there are other ways for doctors to tell if HIV infection has progressed to AIDS. When a person who is HIV-positive develops any of several **indicator diseases**, he or she is said to have AIDS. They are called indicator diseases because they indicate, or show, that a person has AIDS. These diseases can be certain types of cancers, an infection called *PCP* (a type of pneumonia), and tuberculosis (an infection that affects the lungs). Symptoms vary from person to person, but these are some signs that indicate that a person might have AIDS.

New Word

---

indicator disease   n.: one of several diseases that indicate to doctors that a person might have AIDS.

Q A Do people with HIV always get AIDS?

People who are infected with HIV will probably develop AIDS at some point in the future, according to the Centers for Disease Control. The average length of time between infection with HIV and the onset of AIDS is about 7 to 10 years, although some people infected with HIV have remained healthy for a much longer period of time.

Several things determine if and when a person with HIV will develop AIDS:

- People who have poor health habits are more likely to get infections and may develop AIDS sooner. People who eat a balanced diet, get plenty of sleep, and exercise regularly are usually better able to fight off infections.

- Once infected with the virus, infants and children develop AIDS sooner than adults. This is because their immune systems are not as well developed as those of adults. They have a harder time fighting off the virus.

- A person's mental and emotional attitude also can make a difference. Many times, a person with a strong will to live and a positive outlook on life is able to fight off AIDS longer than a person who just gives up after being told he or she has HIV.

Did You Know?

- Diseases associated with AIDS differ from country to country. Even in the United States, the diseases have not stayed the same. For example, when AIDS was first discovered, many people with AIDS got *Kaposi's sarcoma*, a type of skin cancer. This type of cancer is decreasing, but more cases of tuberculosis are showing up in people with AIDS.

- Sometimes when you have the flu, your glands become swollen or enlarged. Swollen glands can also be a symptom of HIV. But with HIV, the glands are swollen in several parts of the body and for no particular reason. Also, the swelling does not go away.

- Another symptom of HIV infection is tiredness or weakness that lasts for a very long time without any explanation.

- The lifetime cost to treat a baby with AIDS in the United States is $418,000.

- A symbol of the fight against AIDS is a loop of red ribbon. This ribbon is worn by people to show support for those who have HIV/AIDS.

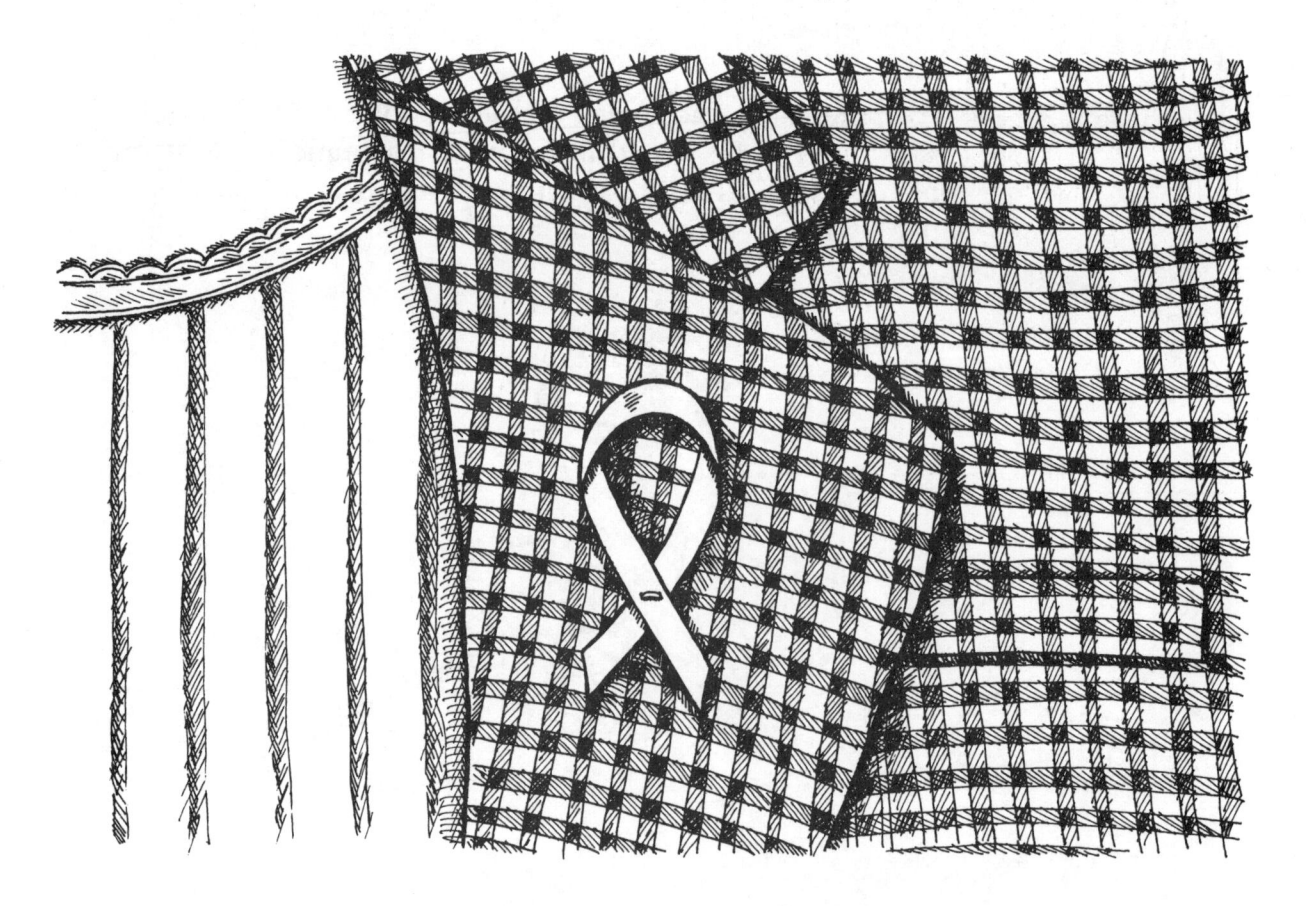

AIDS: First Facts for Kids
© The Learning Works, Inc.

Q Can HIV be prevented?

A
Yes, HIV infection and AIDS can be prevented. Understanding the types of behavior that cause HIV/AIDS is the first step. As you have learned, people who do not have sexual intercourse and who do not use intravenous needles have almost no chance of getting the virus. You can protect yourself from HIV/AIDS by making wise choices for yourself as you enter your teen years. Risky sexual activity and drug abuse are both behaviors that you can control. Remember, once you are infected with HIV, you are infected for the rest of your life.

On Your Own

Design and color a poster to display in your classroom that highlights ways HIV can be prevented.

AIDS: First Facts for Kids
© The Learning Works, Inc.

Q&A What does alcohol and drug use have to do with HIV?

When people use drugs and drink alcoholic beverages, their ability to make good decisions can be affected. They can't always think clearly or act wisely when under the influence of drugs or alcohol.

Sometimes teenagers abuse drugs or drink alcohol at parties. When they do this, they are not in complete control of what they do to others or what other people do to them. They might find themselves in a situation where someone takes sexual advantage of them or they try to do this to others. Don't let yourself be put in this situation! You have control over your own actions. Learn how to say "no" to alcohol and drugs. Here are some examples of ways you can refuse drugs or alcohol in social situations.

Don't go to parties where you know alcohol and/or drugs will be available. If you have a party at your house, don't allow your guests to bring drugs or alcohol.

Associate with friends who don't need alcohol or drugs to have a good time.

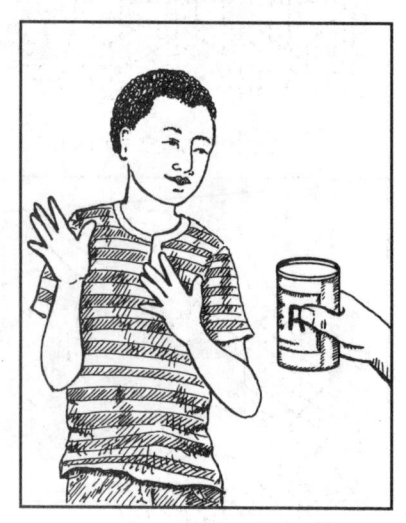

Remember that you don't owe anyone an explanation. Just say "no thanks," and if that doesn't work, make plans to leave the party.

AIDS: First Facts for Kids
© The Learning Works, Inc.

What steps can you take to stay healthy?

Good health habits keep you strong so that your body is better able to resist infections.

Here are some things you can do to stay healthy.

Get plenty of sleep.	Eat a balanced diet.	Avoid substance abuse.
Manage stress effectively.	Exercise regularly.	Love yourself and have a positive outlook on life.

On Your Own Make a list of five health goals you would like to accomplish. Your list might include eating more nutritious foods or exercising more regularly. Read your list over from time to time to see if you are meeting the goals you set for yourself.

Q A How can people reduce their risk of getting AIDS?

You can get AIDS by having sexual intercourse with someone who has the virus even though he or she may not show any symptoms. The surest way for young people to reduce their risk of getting AIDS is not to have sexual intercourse at all.

Later, when you are older and more mature, you will be better able to deal with the physical and emotional aspects of having a close relationship with another person. At that time, it will be important for you to learn about the steps you should take to protect yourself from getting AIDS and other sexually transmitted diseases.

You can also reduce your risk of getting AIDS by not abusing drugs. Never use or share needles.

Care enough about your body to take good care of yourself and not abuse it with drugs. Feel good about yourself, trust your basic instincts about what is right and wrong, and never let yourself be pressured into doing anything you don't want to do. Saying "no" to sex and drugs is the best way to reduce your risk of getting AIDS.

On Your Own

Practice saying "no" to drugs. With a group of classmates, set up role-playing situations where you are offered drugs at school, at a sporting event, at a party, or on the playground. Make up your own dialogue and take turns playing different roles. Think of the many reasons for saying "no" to drugs such as "I care about myself too much to use drugs," or "No thanks, I play sports and would never do that to my body."

AIDS: First Facts for Kids
© The Learning Works, Inc.

What Would You Do?

Discuss or write about what you would do or say in each of the following situations.

- A friend wants to become a "blood brother" or "blood sister" with you. This means you will each cut your finger and have your blood mix. What would you tell your friend?

- Your best friend's younger brother has HIV. Kids at school are afraid of catching HIV from him, so they refuse to touch him or play with him. They don't understand how HIV is transmitted. What would you tell them about the ways in which HIV is transmitted to others?

- You are playing ball at your neighborhood high school over the weekend with some of your friends. A wild ball is thrown on the field and you go to retrieve it. While looking in the bushes for the ball, you find a discarded syringe with the needle still in it. What would you do?

- You and your friends are discussing ways that kids can have a good time without using drugs or alcohol. What are some things you would suggest?

AIDS: First Facts for Kids
© The Learning Works, Inc.

Design a Postage Stamp

Design a unique postage stamp in honor of AIDS awareness. Color your final design with colored marking pens, crayons, or colored pencils.

AIDS: First Facts for Kids
© The Learning Works, Inc.

Topics to Debate

There are many issues that have more than one side when it comes to the topic of HIV/AIDS. With your classmates, debate both sides of the following questions:

- Should the government spend more money on AIDS education and research?

- Should a person be allowed to sue another person for giving him or her HIV?

- Should students infected with HIV be required to tell their classmates that they are HIV-positive?

- Should AIDS testing be required by law?

- Should people in other countries who are infected with HIV be prevented from entering the United States?

- If a vaccine is developed for HIV/AIDS, should all people be required to take the vaccine to prevent passing the virus to others?

AIDS: First Facts for Kids
© The Learning Works, Inc.

Did You Know?

- The AIDS virus can be spread by sharing needles that are used to inject *anabolic steroids*. Steroids are dangerous drugs that are used illegally by some athletes to build their muscles.

- During 1996, an estimated 1.5 million people, including 350,000 children, died from HIV- and AIDS-related illnesses worldwide.

- The only form of completely safe sex is *abstinence*—not having sex at all.

- A *condom* is a sheath of latex rubber that fits over a man's penis. It is used to help prevent semen from entering his partner's body and to prevent his penis from coming in contact with his partner's body fluids.

- Although condoms greatly reduce the chance of HIV infection, they are not completely safe because they can tear or break during sexual intercourse.

- A disease or infection that is spread through sexual contact is called a *sexually transmitted disease* or an *STD*. Examples of STDs are syphilis, herpes, gonorrhea, and AIDS.

What should people do if they test positive for HIV?

People who test positive for HIV should be helped by trained counselors. Counselors help people deal with the fear and anger they may feel upon learning that they have become infected with HIV. People who test positive for HIV are advised to see a doctor as soon as possible so medical care can begin. They are usually advised to get plenty of rest, exercise on a regular basis, eat healthy foods, and avoid stress. Many people who find out they have HIV join a support group with other people who have HIV. In the group meetings, they share their thoughts and feelings and exchange ideas and information. They are also taught precautions to prevent them from infecting anyone else.

On Your Own

Find out what services are available in your community to help people who test positive for HIV. See if there are things you can do to help these organizations. For example, with the assistance of a teacher or other adult, you could hold a fundraiser with a group of your friends and donate the money collected to an organization that helps people with HIV/AIDS.

AIDS: First Facts for Kids
© The Learning Works, Inc.

Q A Is there a cure for AIDS?

No. One of the most frightening things about AIDS is that scientists do not know of a treatment that will kill the human immunodeficiency virus once it enters the body. There is no cure that will restore the immune system once it has been damaged or destroyed. People with HIV are infected for life. As long as they live, they are capable of transmitting this virus to other people.

Researchers are working to find a cure for HIV/AIDS. In the meantime, they are looking for more effective ways of controlling HIV/AIDS symptoms in people who have **contracted** the disease. Researchers are also looking for a vaccine that will prevent those who are not yet infected from getting HIV.

New Word

contract (ken-trakt) v.: to acquire without wanting or trying to.

Q&A What drugs are available to treat HIV/AIDS?

As of this writing, there are no vaccines that have been approved to prevent HIV infection. There are, however, drugs that have been developed to help slow the rate at which the virus reproduces and to treat some of the opportunistic infections related to HIV.

The first drug developed to help fight HIV was **AZT**. It cannot kill the virus, but it can slow the rate at which the virus reproduces. However, after a patient has been on this type of drug for several months, different strains of HIV develop that are resistant to AZT. This means that the AZT will no longer work. Therefore, doctors now use a combination of medicines to treat the infection more effectively. The combination of several drugs has been found to strengthen and lengthen the beneficial effects of AZT.

Drugs have also been developed to treat the infections that are associated with AIDS and to help the body's immune system work better. One drug is called *Interferon*. Interferon helps fight certain types of cancers that people with AIDS often get.

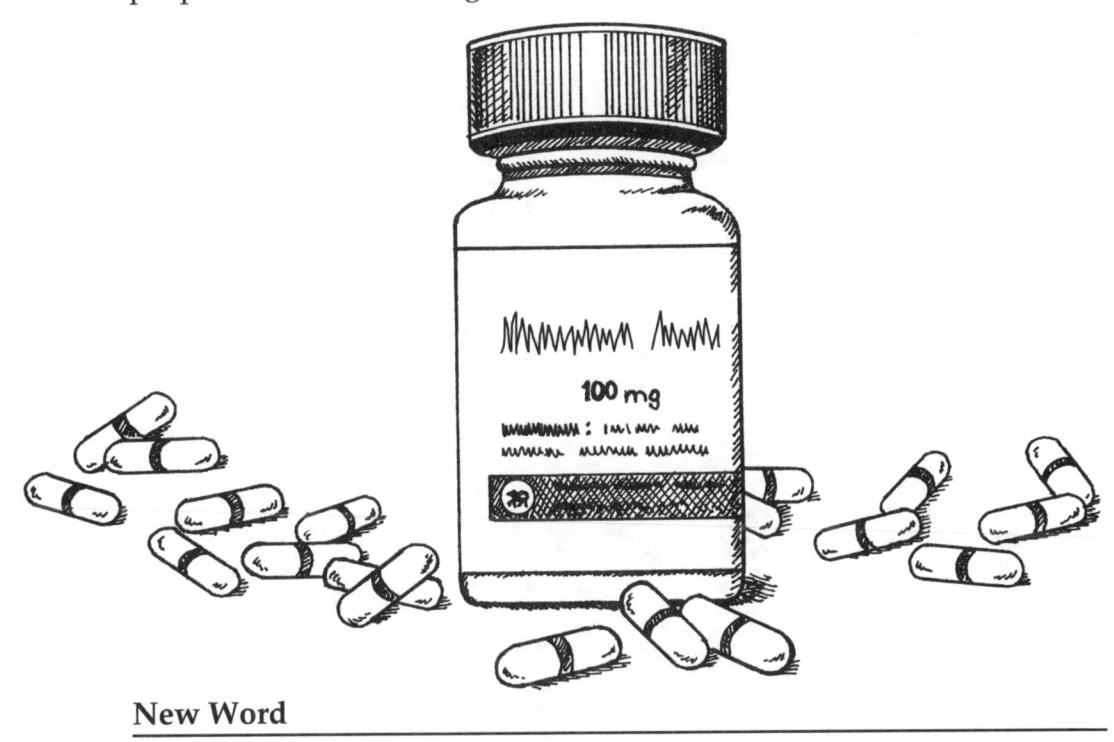

New Word

AZT n.: a drug given to HIV patients that slows the rate at which the virus reproduces.

AIDS: First Facts for Kids
© The Learning Works, Inc.

Did You Know?

- Many cities have clinics where free, anonymous, HIV-antibody tests are given to those who want to be tested.

- After becoming infected with HIV, it takes the body two weeks to six months to build up enough antibodies to be detected by a blood test. This period of time is called the *window period*. During this window period, a person can still infect another person if he or she has sex or shares drug needles.

- Certain groups of people are routinely tested for HIV. These include immigrants entering the United States; people in the foreign service, such as Peace Corps volunteers and diplomats; and men and women applying to the armed forces or Job Corps.

- In addition to the treatments and medications doctors prescribe, some people try alternative treatments such as vitamin therapy, special diets, and the use of herbs to fight AIDS.

Did You Know?

- If researchers developed a vaccine against HIV tomorrow and everyone in the world received this vaccine immediately, the number of new AIDS cases would still grow for at least five years or more because so many people have already been infected with HIV and will eventually develop AIDS.

- Scientists are currently studying *gene transfer therapy* as a method of treating HIV. In this type of therapy, genes are transferred to healthy cells to make them resistant to HIV infection.

- One type of drug used to fight HIV infection is called a *protease inhibitor*. This drug reduces the amount of HIV in a person's blood by stopping the action of certain enzymes called *proteases* that the virus needs to replicate or duplicate itself.

- Even though there is no cure for AIDS, it is important for people who test positive for HIV to get medical treatment as soon as possible. Prompt medical care may delay the onset of AIDS and prevent some opportunistic infections that can be life threatening.

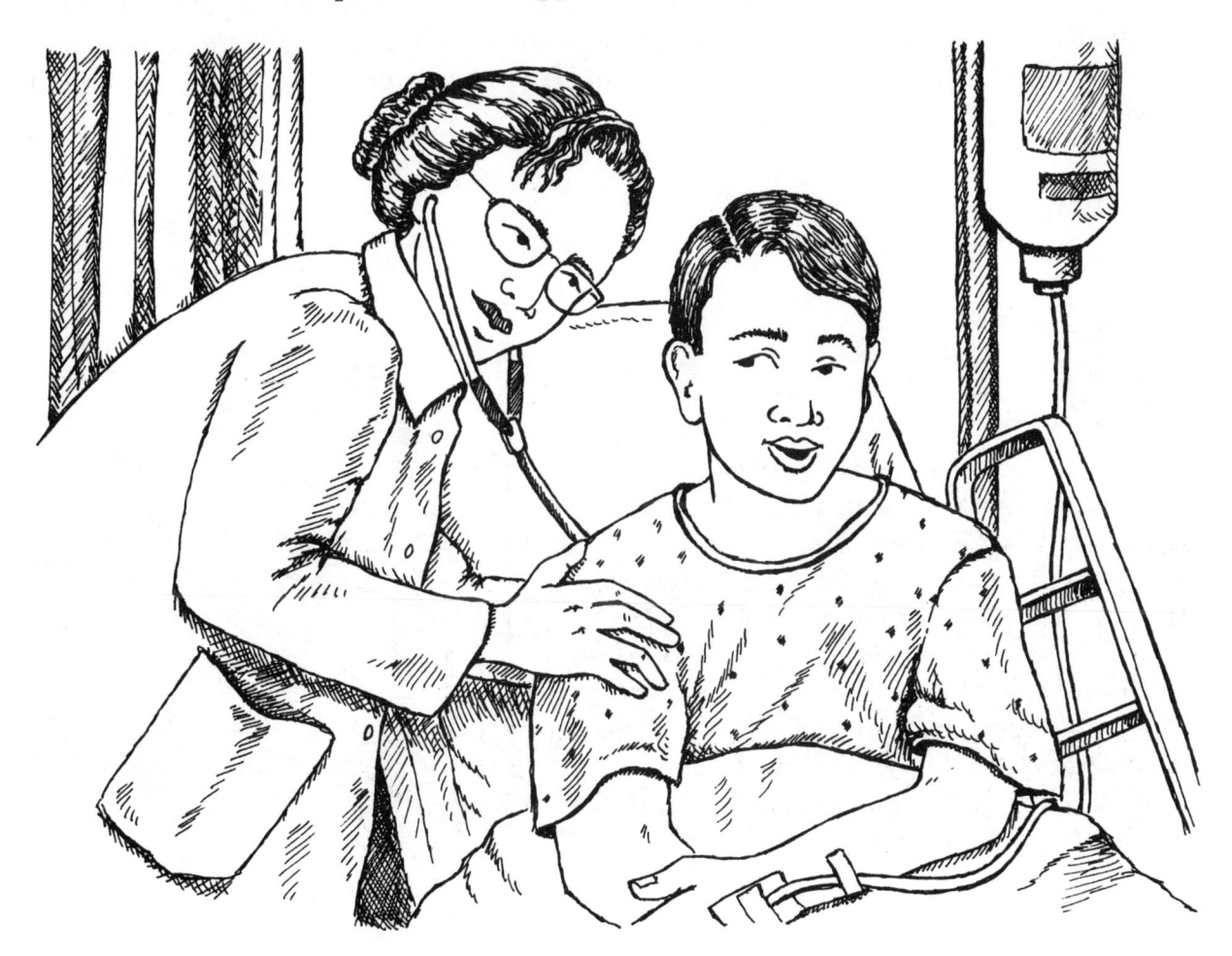

People in Profile

Ryan White

Ryan White was a young boy who had hemophilia. Hemophilia is a disease where a person lacks certain factors that make the blood clot properly. Ryan needed blood product transfusions to help his blood clot, otherwise he could bleed excessively from even a minor injury. Ryan was infected with HIV by a blood transfusion he received before the nation's blood supply was screened for the virus. When Ryan was thirteen, he was banned from attending his local school in Kokomo, Indiana, because he was infected with HIV. He and his family moved to Cicero, Indiana, where he was given a lot of support and was made to feel welcomed by the students and faculty. Ryan spoke about AIDS to students in other schools and also spoke before the President's Commission on AIDS. Ryan White died in 1990 at the age of eighteen from complications due to AIDS. He not only fought HIV but also fought for his right to attend school and to be treated with respect and dignity.

Arthur Ashe

Arthur Ashe became the first African American to win a Grand Slam tennis title when he won the 1968 U.S. Open. Like Ryan White, Arthur contracted HIV through a blood transfusion. He received the transfusion during a heart operation in 1983. At first, after learning he was HIV-positive, Arthur Ashe didn't tell anyone else that he was infected. But eventually he made an announcement that he had contracted the virus. He then became a leading spokesperson in telling the public about AIDS. Arthur Ashe died of AIDS-related causes in 1993.

AIDS: First Facts for Kids
© The Learning Works, Inc.

Q&A How does society treat people who have HIV/AIDS?

Sometimes people are afraid to get close to a person who has HIV/AIDS because they are worried about catching the virus. Many of these people do not realize that HIV/AIDS is hard to get. They do not understand that they can't catch HIV/AIDS by touching or being in close contact with someone who is infected. As a result, many people with HIV/AIDS feel alone and rejected at a time when they need extra care, support, and love. Remember, it is the disease itself that is bad, not the person who has HIV/AIDS. A person who has HIV/AIDS needs the warmth and love of family and friends who care at a time when he or she may be feeling very lonely and sick.

AIDS: First Facts for Kids
© The Learning Works, Inc.

Q A What can you do to help someone with HIV/AIDS?

Often people feel helpless and don't know what to do for a person who has HIV/AIDS. Here are some suggestions for ways you can help someone who has AIDS or another serious illness.

- Write or send a letter or card to the person with HIV/AIDS. Have fun illustrating your letter or card with drawings or stickers.

- Offer to do a task for the person with HIV/AIDS, such as writing a letter, walking a pet, running an errand, watering plants, or fixing a meal.

- Send your favorite jokes or riddles each week.

- If you visit a person who is sick in a hospital or at home, bring magazines or books for him or her to read.

- Offer to clean the person's cupboards, organize their kitchen pantry, or help with other household chores because he or she may not feel well enough to take care of these things.

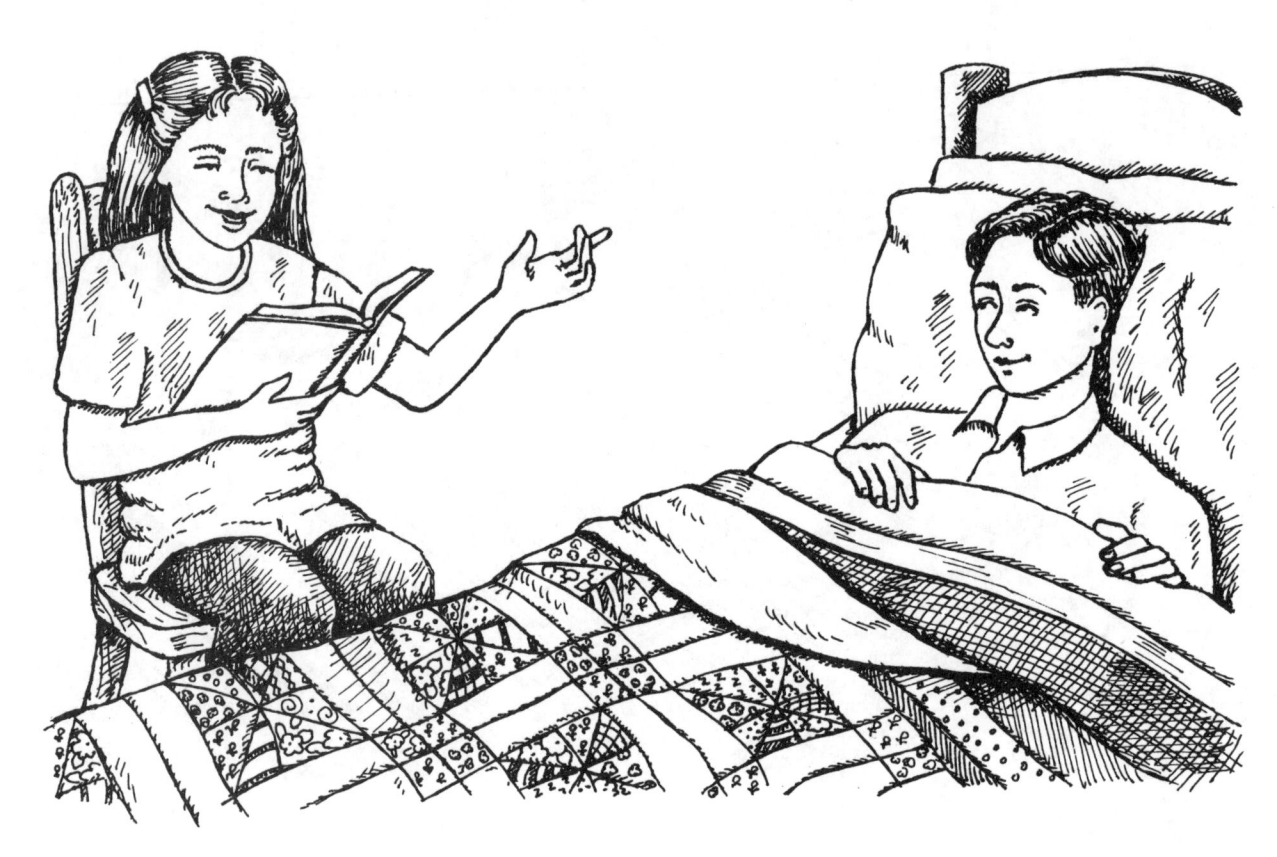

AIDS: First Facts for Kids
© The Learning Works, Inc.

What can you do to help someone with HIV/AIDS? (continued)

- Read aloud to a person with HIV/AIDS from his or her favorite book, a collection of poetry, a newspaper, or a magazine.

- Make a bath basket for a person who is sick and fill it with bubble bath, scented soaps, a wash cloth, and a bath sponge.

- Mow the lawn or rake the leaves for a person with HIV/AIDS.

- Pack a picnic lunch for someone who is ill and enjoy it together at a park or at the beach. (Many people who are HIV-positive must follow a special diet, so ask the person in advance what foods you should bring.)

- Offer to play a game of cards, checkers, chess, or other board game to help entertain someone who is sick.

- Bake a batch of homemade cookies and bring them to your friend.

- Be there for your friend. A simple squeeze of the hand or a hug lets him or her know you care.

AIDS: First Facts for Kids
© The Learning Works, Inc.

How have your feelings changed?

After completing this unit on HIV/AIDS, see if your original beliefs and attitudes have changed. This survey is just for you; you don't have to share it with anyone else. It will help you see how much you have learned and how that knowledge has affected your beliefs about HIV/AIDS. On a separate piece of paper, write short answers or "yes" or "no" responses.

1. Did the information in this unit make you more aware of HIV/AIDS?

2. Did the information presented change your attitude about this disease? If so, how?

3. Did you learn new facts about:
   - HIV, the virus that causes AIDS?
   - the ways in which HIV is transmitted to other people?
   - how to protect yourself from this disease?
   - HIV testing?
   - the symptoms of AIDS?
   - how doctors and counselors help people who have tested positive for HIV?

4. Did the information presented in this unit change your thinking about your future sexual behavior? If so, how?

5. Did the information presented in this unit change your thinking about the use of drugs and alcohol? If so, how?

6. Did the information you learned about HIV change your feelings about people with HIV/AIDS? If so, how?

AIDS: First Facts for Kids
© The Learning Works, Inc.

Word Search Puzzle

The twelve AIDS-related terms listed here have been hidden among the letters in the box below. As you search for them, remember to read up, down, and diagonally—backwards as well as forwards.

AIDS	DISEASE	IMMUNE	TRANSFUSION
ANTIBODIES	EPIDEMIC	INTRAVENOUS	VACCINE
BLOOD	HIV	SEMEN	VIRUS

```
T X V U I M M U N E V B
I R W V I R U S R P A Q
B E A I D S T Z O N C X
C P G N C S H J T N C J
G I F O S K E I M B I Y
H D A D L F B M Y A N W
V E E M K O U S E M E N
A M N O D S H S C N L O
Y I D I C U I B I R G K
G C E A B R V B L O O D
D S D I S E A S E M N A
I N T R A V E N O U S B
```

AIDS: First Facts for Kids
© The Learning Works, Inc.

The AIDS Quilt

The Names Project AIDS Memorial Quilt was first displayed in Washington, D.C., in October, 1987. The quilt is made up of panels that have been donated by individuals and families who have lost a loved one to AIDS. Each panel measures three feet by six feet and contains the person's name and something special about him or her. It might be pictures of things the person especially liked to do, places he or she visited, his or her pets, or messages of love from friends and relatives. It is a way family and friends can honor the person who has died and can capture some of the special qualities that made that person unique.

The quilt now has more than 33,000 panels and stretches over 15 acres. It covers an area the size of eight football fields and weighs more than 16 tons. It is so large that it can't be displayed in one location. Instead, parts of the quilt are sometimes displayed at special events across the country.

On Your Own

- A personal letter written by friends and/or family accompanies each panel of the AIDS Quilt. If you are interested in reading some of these letters, locate the following book at your public library: *A Promise to Remember: The NAMES Project Book of Letters* by Joe Brown (Avon, 1992).

- Another popular program is the Children's Quilt Project. This program was started in 1988 in Berkeley, California. The purpose of the Children's Quilt Project is to make and supply warm quilts for children with AIDS. Find out if your community has a support program like this and make a class quilt you can donate to show your support for children who have AIDS.

AIDS: First Facts for Kids
© The Learning Works, Inc.

An AIDS Review

How much have you learned about HIV/AIDS? Fill in the blanks or circle the best answer or the most appropriate response.

1. The acronym AIDS stands for

   _____ _____ _____ _____

2. AIDS is caused by
   a. antibodies
   b. bacteria
   c. a virus
   d. germs in the air

3. The most common way to find out if a person has been infected with HIV is to
   a. take the person's blood pressure
   b. check the person's urine
   c. determine the person's heart rate
   d. test the person's blood for the presence of HIV antibodies

4. HIV is found in the largest amounts in which body fluid?
   a. saliva
   b. blood
   c. tears
   d. breast milk

Write **T** on the line in front of each statement that is true. Write **F** on the line in front of each statement that is false.

_____ 5. Scientists have developed a test to determine if a person has AIDS.

_____ 6. HIV stays in the bloodstream for life.

_____ 7. HIV attacks the body's white blood cells.

_____ 8. A person can become infected with HIV by sharing a meal with an AIDS patient.

_____ 9. An adult is said to have AIDS if his or her CD4-cell count is below 1,000.

_____ 10. A person can become infected with HIV by having sexual intercourse with someone who is infected with HIV.

_____ 11. A person can become infected with HIV by sharing intravenous needles with an HIV-infected person.

_____ 12. Doctors have recently developed a drug to cure AIDS.

AIDS: First Facts for Kids
© The Learning Works, Inc.

Research Projects

- As a class, make plans to interview a nurse, doctor, or authority on AIDS to learn more about this disease. Begin by brainstorming a list of questions you want to ask. Then invite the guest to your class for the interview. You may wish to tape your interview.

- Create a game to test your classmates' knowledge about HIV and AIDS. Cover a shoe box with colored construction paper. Decorate the box with newspaper headlines about AIDS. Using 3" x 5" index cards, list 15 facts you have learned about HIV and AIDS, writing only one fact per card. Then, make up three false statements and write them on three separate cards. Mix the cards up and number them from 1 through 18. Place these numbered cards in your decorated shoe box. See if your classmates can correctly identify the three false statements. It's a good idea to make an answer key. Tape an envelope to the inside of the shoe box lid. Write the card numbers of the three false facts on an index card. Place this card inside the envelope where your classmates can use it to check their answers.

- Polio is another infectious disease caused by a virus. Before 1954, the year in which Jonas Salk developed the first vaccine for the prevention of polio, many people were hospitalized each summer with this disease. Many had severe cases that crippled or killed them. Ask your parents or grandparents what they remember about polio. Did they know someone who had polio? What precautions did they take to avoid catching this disease? How did they feel when a vaccine finally became available? Based on your research, compare AIDS with polio. In what ways are these viral diseases similar? In what ways are they different?

- Search the Internet and find 10 new facts about HIV/AIDS. Here are some Web sites that have information to help you:

    http://www.cdcnac.org
    http://www.aacap.org/web/aacap/factsFam/aids.htm
    http://www.ryanwhite.org/

- To stay current with the latest information, research, and new drugs for HIV/AIDS, collect newspaper and magazine articles about these topics. Write a brief summary in your own words for each article. Share your summaries with your classmates on a class bulletin board.

Creative Writing and Art Ideas

Creative Writing

- Write a letter to a friend, real or fictional, expressing your support after learning that he or she has contracted HIV.

- Write a letter to the editor of your local paper telling why you think the government should spend more (or less) money on AIDS research. Before you write your letter, do research to see how much money is currently being spent annually.

- Write a poem about HIV or AIDS. Your poem does not have to rhyme.

- Write a short story in which you describe the discrimination a person with HIV or AIDS might experience.

Art

- Design a poster for a "National AIDS Awareness Week." Create a slogan for your poster. Illustrate your poster using colored marking pens, crayons, or paints.

- From a sheet of white art paper, cut a circle three inches in diameter. Then, design a logo and a slogan appropriate for an AIDS awareness campaign at an elementary school. Draw your logo on the button and color it. Add your slogan in neat, clear lettering.

- Draw a cartoon or comic strip to illustrate one important fact about AIDS.

Role-Playing Activities

People who test positive for HIV are faced not only with a life-threatening illness but with other serious problems as well. Many of these people lose their jobs and nearly all of them will have increased medical expenses. Sometimes their friends and family members ignore them or treat them unkindly.

- Role-play a situation with your classmates where a person is discriminated against at work, at home, or at school because he or she tests positive for HIV.

- Role-play a situation where a student at school is afraid to touch or get close to another student who has HIV. In your dialogue, bring out the important facts you learned about how the virus is passed on to others and how it is **not** passed on.

- Your older brother is using intravenous drugs. You know that HIV can be transmitted through improperly sterilized syringes and needles. You are concerned for your brother's health and safety and have decided to confront him. Role-play your conversation. Ask a classmate to play the role of your brother. Then trade places and switch roles.

- You don't think enough money is being spent on finding a cure for HIV/AIDS. Your friend disagrees and thinks that less money should be spent on AIDS and more money should be spent on cancer research. Role-play a conversation with another classmate in which each of you support your beliefs.

- You and a friend disagree about the advantages and disadvantages of being tested for HIV. Role-play your conversation.

Cooperative Projects

Research has taught us a lot about how HIV is transmitted. There is a continuing need for additional research to discover how this disease can be prevented, treated, and cured. Money is needed to conduct this research and to care for persons who are ill with the disease. You can help!

With your classmates, plan an event to help raise money for AIDS research, education, or patient care. Consider having a bake sale, a bike-a-thon, a rummage sale, a used book sale, or another type of fundraiser. Organize committees to help with the planning, advertising, publicity, ticket sales, and/or cleanup.

Books to Read

Dever, Barbara Christie. *AIDS: Answers to Questions Kids Ask*, The Learning Works, Inc. Santa Barbara, CA, 1996. (Grades 6–8)

Ford, Michael Thomas. *One Hundred Questions and Answers About AIDS: A Guide for Young People*, Macmillan Publishing Company, New York, NY, 1992.

Hyde, Margaret O., and Forsyth, Elizabeth H. *Know About AIDS*, Walker and Company, New York, NY, 1994.

Manning, Karen. *AIDS: Can This Epidemic Be Stopped?* Henry Holt and Company, New York, 1995.

Sirimarco, Elizabeth. *AIDS*, Marshall Cavendish Corporation, New York, 1994.

Taylor, Barbara. *Everything You Need to Know About AIDS*, The Rosen Publishing Group, New York, NY, 1992.

Westheimer, Dr. Ruth. *Dr. Ruth Talks to Kids*, Macmillan Publishing Company, New York, NY, 1993.

Biographies and novels about people with AIDS

Fox, Paula. *The Eagle Kite*, Orchard Books, New York, NY, 1995.

Kittredge, Mary. *Teens With AIDS Speak Out*, Thorndike Press, Thorndike, ME, 1991.

Landau, Elaine. *We Have AIDS*, Franklin Watts, Inc., New York, NY, 1990.

White, Ryan, and Cunningham, Ann Marie. *Ryan White: My Own Story*, Dial Books, Division of Penguin Books USA Inc., 1991.

Resources for More Information

Many groups are trying to help people learn more about HIV/AIDS. You can write to any of the agencies, associations, and foundations listed below. Because most of them are nonprofit groups, their funds to cover postage and handling are limited. For this reason, you should enclose a self-addressed stamped envelope with each request.

AIDS Action Council
1875 Connecticut Ave., N.W., Suite 700
Washington, DC 20009

American Foundation for AIDS Research
733 Third Avenue, Twelfth Floor
New York, NY 10017

American Red Cross
Office of HIV/AIDS Education
1709 New York Avenue, N.W., Suite 208
Washington, DC 20006

Canadian Public Health Association
AIDS Education Awareness Program
National AIDS Clearing House
1565 Carling Avenue, Suite 400
Ottawa, Ontario, Canada K1Z 8R1

CDC National AIDS Clearing House
P.O. Box 6003
Rockville, MD 20849

HIV/AIDS Treatment Information Service
P.O. Box 6303
Rockville, MD 20849

National Institutes of Health
Office of AIDS Research
Building 31, Room 5C-06
Bethesda, MD 20892

Resources for More Information

If your need for information is urgent, you can call one or more of the hotlines listed below and receive immediate attention. When you call, trained personnel will answer your questions and tell you where you can obtain additional information. Since some of these numbers are toll calls for which you will be charged a fee, get permission from one of your parents before placing any calls.

AIDS and Cancer Research Foundation Hotline
1-800-373-4572

AIDS Project Los Angeles
1-213-993-1600

American Institute for Teen AIDS Prevention
1-817-237-0230

HIV/AIDS Treatment Information Service
1-800-448-0440

Los Angeles Pediatric AIDS Network (LAPAN)
1-213-669-5616

National AIDS Clearing House
1-800-458-5231

CDC National AIDS Hotline
1-800-342-2437
1-800-344-7432 (in Spanish)
1-800-243-7889 (hearing-impaired)

Teens Teaching AIDS Prevention
1-800-234-TEEN

Youth Development International
1-800-HIT-HOME

Answer Key

Word Search Puzzle • Page 47

Page 49 • An AIDS Review
1. acquired immune deficiency syndrome
2. c
3. d
4. b
5. F
6. T
7. T
8. F
9. F
10. T
11. T
12. F

AIDS: First Facts for Kids
© The Learning Works, Inc.